General Tom Thumb and his Lady

by
Mertie E. Romaine

Published By
WILLIAM S. SULLWOLD PUBLISHING, INC.
Taunton, Massachusetts

ISBN 0-88492-018-6 Hard Cover
ISBN 0-88492-019-4 Paper Cover
LCCCN 76-53594

Printed in the United States

FOREWORD

The author has been fascinated by the Tom Thumbs ever since she was a young girl and all her life has collected material and memorabilia of the famous little people. When in her teens, she was frequently invited to the home of neighbors, Mr. and Mrs. Allerton Thompson, where Mrs. Tom Thumb (then Countess Magri) was also a frequent visitor. The host would lift Lavinia onto a table in the center of the parlor and there she would stand and sing songs and deliver recitations all from memory in her incredibly sweet and childish voice. As she stood beside the author, Lavinia's head reached just to the author's waist, barely a yard tall.

Mrs. Tom Thumb was born in Middleborough, Massachusetts and every summer after the show season was over, the General and his wife would spend the summer at their home in Middleborough. For these reasons, the residents of the town have a kind of proprietary interest in all that pertains to the Tom Thumbs, and it seems particularly appropriate that the largest collection of Tom Thumb memorabilia is located in Lavinia's home town.

Mertie E. Romaine

April, 1976

In Arthur's court Tom Thumb did live,
    A man of mickle might,
The best of all the table round
    And he a doughty knight;
His stature but an inch in height,
    Or quarter of a span;
Then think you not this little knight
    Was proved a valiant man?

             Nursery Rhyme

CONTENTS

THE GENERAL AND HIS LADY

Chapter I
INTRODUCING
THE WORLD'S MOST FAMOUS MIDGETS
GENERAL AND MRS. TOM THUMB

On a crisp October morning in the year 1841, a baby girl was born who was destined to win fame and fortune far beyond her dimunitive size. This event took place on October 31, 1841, in the pleasant New England village of Middleborough, Massachusetts, at the gateway to Cape Cod. The parents named their infant daughter Mercy Lavinia Warren Bump.

James S. and Huldah P. Bump were the parents of seven children: four boys, George, James, Sylvanus, and Benjamin, all of whom grew to a height of six feet and more; three girls: Mercy Lavinia and Huldah (later known as Minnie Warren), neither of whom ever grew taller than a yardstick, and Caroline Delia, who became a normal sized person and married Homer Warren Southworth of Midleborough. Huldah was born June 2, 1849, eight years after Lavinia's birth, and when full grown reached only to Lavinia's shoulder.

The bewildered parents watched and worried as their daughter Lavinia grew in years but not in stature. After she gained the age of four she never added another inch to her height. At nine years of age Lavinia entered school, a one-room schoolhouse not far from her home. Her tiny legs could not keep up with her schoolmates and they took turns carrying her on their shoulders, in winter pulling her behind them on a sled. All the children loved their tiny playmate and vied with one another for the privilege of carrying her. As long as she lived,

LAVINIA'S BIRTHPLACE
Plymouth Street, Middleboro

Lavinia delighted in telling of the many times the teacher stood her up on a desk to sing for the other pupils, and in later years the pupils took equal pleasure in recalling that as Lavinia stood upon the desk and sang her songs she resembled nothing as much as a lovely animated doll.

Lavinia was not long in discovering she could vary the routine of school life by trotting up and down the aisles quite unobserved by the schoolmaster. When discovered in her mischief the schoolmaster threatened to put her in his shoe. Soon Lavinia thought of another method to enliven the day. The old-fashioned desks were open underneath and by ducking her small head the wee midget could easily walk the entire length of the room unseen. She became the bearer of notes from one scholar to another. At last the exasperated schoolmaster seated her on the largest dictionary he could find; at least he could keep his eye on the top of Lavinia's head.

Unusually intelligent, Lavinia soon discovered she knew more than the teacher. She withdrew from school and employed her time learning from her mother how to cook, sew, and care for a home.

One day when she was sixteen years old, Lavinia received a caller, a gentleman who proved to be a relative, and had financial interests in showboats on the Mississippi River. He

THE WOMEN IN THE BUMP FAMILY
Lavinia, Caroline Delia, Mrs. Bump, Minnie

made the startling suggestion that Lavinia join his traveling shows on the Spaulding & Rogers Show Boats, great flat-boats that presented daily performances as they plied up and down the river. At first Lavinia's father and mother were strongly opposed to such a proposition, but when they were assured their daughter would always have a woman companion, they gave their consent. Lavinia herself was eager to go, eager to travel and meet people.

After four years of traveling in the west, Lavinia returned to her home in Middleborough and despite her size, was engaged to teach in the one-room country school she had attended in her youth. Most of her pupils were taller than their teacher, but possessing a dignity that made up for her lack of inches, Lavinia had little trouble with discipline. She was thus employed when P. T. Barnum, the great American showman, heard about her and lost no time in traveling to Middleborough to investigate the possibilities of engaging her to appear in his American Museum in New York City, where he had collected and was exhibiting astounding curiosities, human and otherwise, from all over the world.

THE BUMP FAMILY HOMESTEAD
Plymouth Street, Middleboro

Among the most popular of the exhibits at the Museum
were two little midgets, General Tom Thumb and Commodore
Nutt. Mr. Barnum, with his uncanny showman's instinct, could
clearly visualize the advantages to be gained by the added attraction of a young woman of the same diminutive size. Considerable persuasion was necessary to overcome Mr. and Mrs.
Bump's aversion to the idea of their daughter again becoming
a public spectacle. A contract was finally signed with the stip-
ulation that Lavinia be known as Lavinia Warren, her mother's
maiden name, since Mr. Barnum did not consider the name of
Bump glamorous enough for show business. Mr. Barnum took
Lavinia off to New York to purchase costumes and jewelry for
her debut at the Museum.

While in New York, Lavinia stayed at the St. Nicholas
Hotel where she was visited by hundreds of the curious, the
elite of society and newspaper representatives. All were
amazed to find her a perfectly formed woman in minature,
beautiful, charming, lovable, and a brilliant conversationalist.
New York lost its heart to her. The New York Sun of December 23, 1862, had this to say about the visitor:

"There is a little lady at the St. Nicholas Hotel who bids fair to throw the career of Tom Thumb and the efforts of the great Barnum himself, in dwarf proportions, entirely in the shade. This miniature queen of the Lilliputs is but 32 inches high, 21 years old, and of excellent form. Her dresses are magnificent, being clothed at the rate of $2000 per outfit, and sparkling with jewels and splendor. Many would deem it a show to see the dresses, but dresses and contents together are a little ahead of anything which tiny hoops have enclosed for many a year."

LOVELY LAVINIA
In young womanhood

GENERAL TOM THUMB

"The American Man in Miniature. He is smaller than any infant that ever walked alone. Is 25 inches high and weighs only 15 pounds." Lithograph by J. Baillie.

12

Lavinia was now ready to make her appearance at the American Museum and join Mr. Barnum's stellar attraction, General Tom Thumb. In November, 1842, while visiting his brother in Bridgeport, Connecticut, Mr. Barnum had heard of a tiny child who was at the age of four not quite twenty-eight inches high and weighed less than six pounds. At Mr. Barnum's request, his brother brought the child to see him. The tiny tot was indeed amazing. He promptly told Mr. Barnum his name, Charles Sherwood Stratton, and that his father's name was Sherwood Stratton.

Mr. Barnum saw at once the financial possibilities of adding this little phenomenon to the attractions at the American Museum. Arrangements were made with the child's parents to engage him at three dollars per week for four weeks, all living and traveling expenses for both the boy and his mother to be paid by Mr. Barnum.

Always ready with an apt sobriquet for members of his unusual company, Mr. Barnum dubbed the newest member, "General Tom Thumb," and arranged his debut at the Museum for Thanksgiving Day, celebrated in 1842 on December 8th. Much of the time of the first four weeks was spent in educating and training Tom Thumb, who proved to be a keen, intelligent pupil, quickly comprehending the instructions given him. At the end of four weeks, a new contract was arranged for one year at seven dollars a week, with a bonus of fifty dollars at the expiration of twelve months.

With his never failing acuity, Mr. Barnum realized that an attraction imported from England would have far greater drawing power than one from nearby Connecticut, and that the boy's size would appear all the more remarkable if the public were led to believe he was older than his actual age. Therefore handbills were distributed advertising the new discovery as "a wonderful dwarf of eleven years of age, just arrived from England."

Thousands flocked to see this little, but great, curiosity. His levees at all hours were crowded. General Tom Thumb greeted the throngs in the reception hall of the Museum, and after calling attention to the beautiful fountain and to the other curiosities on exhibition, he ascended a platform in the great

13

P. T. BARNUM AND THE FAMOUS MIDGETS
General and Mrs. Tom Thumb

hall on the third floor where the stage was set with his miniature furniture and a tiny carriage with Shetland ponies.

The exhibition he presented consisted of skits and tab-
leaux in which he appeared in costume. First saluting the
audience, he was lifted to a chair and sang in a high, sweet
voice a patriotic selection. After this, acknowledging the enthusiastic applause with a deep bow, he retired from the stage,
reappearing in a different costume for the first of his impersonations.

Off stage, Tom was sartorial perfection. His boots were
Wellingtons made of fine, soft kid; his suits were the product
of distinguished tailors; and his gloves so small the fingers
were but one and one-half inches long. Strutting about the
stage, swinging a tiny cane, his head level with the seats of
the chairs, he did indeed represent a sight that had to be seen
to be believed. As long as he lived, the General's voice was a
childish treble. It could not be expected that such tiny vocal
chords could produce the full voice of manhood.

Always looking for new worlds to conquer, Mr. Barnum
made a contract for General Tom Thumb's services at fifty
dollars a week with permission to exhibit him in Europe. Ac-
cordingly, on January 19, 1844, Mr. Barnum and the General,
accompanied by Tom's parents and a tutor, sailed from New
York for Liverpool.

Preceded by word of his fame, the party was greeted in
Liverpool by a great crowd collected on the dock to catch a
glimpse of this extraordinary visitor from America. The throng
was doomed to disappointment as Mrs. Stratton picked up the
General in her arms and carried him ashore like a baby.

Prospects of success in Europe were at first not encourag-
ing. The initial offer received for exhibiting Tom Thumb was
made by the proprietor of a wax works at ten dollars a week.
Mr. Barnum still had high hopes of presenting his protege to
their Majesties at Buckingham Palace and was delighted when
he received word that the manager of the Princess Theatre in
London was coming to witness a performance in the hall in
Liverpool that Mr. Barnum had engaged for a short season.
The manager, Mr. Maddox, was favorably impressed with Tom
Thumb's performance and engaged him for three nights at the

Princess Theatre. Thus an opening wedge was established that might lead to an appearance before the elite of London and, with good fortune, to Buckingham Palace.

People clamored to see the American curiosity, but Barnum was not to be stampeded. He wished to make the most of this golden opportunity. Renting a large furnished house on Bond Street, the center of fashionable society, he sent invitations to representatives of the press, nobility, and men and women of high station in English life. These invitations to meet General Tom Thumb were much sought after and many applied for admission who could not be accommodated.

The tide had turned. An engagement in Egyptian Hall in Picadilly met with unqualified success. Shortly after came the coveted invitation from Queen Victoria, having been instigated by the efforts of Ambassador Everett and Mr. Charles Murray, Master of the Queen's Household. To capitalize on this event, a notice was posted on the door of Egyptian Hall, "Closed this evening, General Tom Thumb being at Buckingham Palace by Command of Her Majesty."

The Queen and royal party received the Americans in the picture gallery of the palace. The great doors were thrown open and Tom Thumb advanced looking like an animated doll. Approaching the royal group, he made a deep bow and said, as he always greeted his audiences, "Good evening, ladies and gentlemen." This was greeted by laughter and the smiling Queen led her tiny guest by the hand about the gallery, after which he presented his repertoire of songs and recitations.

The entertainment lasted an hour, after which came time for departure, which proved to have slight regard for court protocol. The withdrawal began according to instructions, a few backward steps punctuated with a respectful bow. Mr. Barnum's long legs covered the ground much faster than the General's tiny limbs. Glancing back every few steps and perceiving the distance growing between them, Tom Thumb would turn and run to catch up with his companion, turn again and bow toward the Queen, then once more run to catch up with Mr. Barnum. It was a ludicrous performance and the royal spectators were convulsed with laughter.

All this confusion was too much for the Queen's King Charles spaniel, which entered into the fun by chasing Tom and nipping at his heels. Tom halted his running long enough to wave his little cane in an attempt to ward off the barking dog. The royal party threw all dignity to the winds and joined in unrestrained mirth. When one considers that at this time Tom was only six years old instead of the thirteen years claimed by Mr. Barnum, his behavior was far more creditable than it might appear.

The audience before Queen Victoria brought the desired results; the exhibitions of General Tom Thumb became so crowded it was necessary to move to a larger hall. Two other command performances were given at Buckingham Palace. On each occasion Mr. Barnum carried along the tiny upholstered sofa which always accompanied Tom Thumb so he would have a comfortable seat and not have to perch on a high and uncomfortable piece of furniture. Later, when there were four little people in the troupe, the sofa and two tiny chairs upholstered in red velvet to match the sofa traveled with them around the world.

The Queen presented Tom Thumb with many costly gifts, including a tiny card case of mother-of-pearl mounted with gold and precious stones, ornamented on one side with the crown and royal initials, and on the other with a bouquet of flowers in enamel and jewels. In this card case the General kept his Lilliputian calling cards which he delighted in distributing at every opportunity. Later Queen Victoria presented the Tom Thumbs with a little grand piano. One of the tiny sewing machines Mrs. Tom Thumb owned was said to have been a present from the Queen. The most famous of all the gifts from Queen Victoria was the little coach drawn by four tiny Shetland ponies. In this coach, with a tiny coachman perched high on the driver's seat, General and Mrs. Tom Thumb rode triumphantly through each town and city in which they gave exhibitions.

After each performance at Buckingham Palace, a sizable sum of money was given to Mr. Barnum, but no amount of money could equal the advantage gained from these appearances before the Queen. Attendance at the exhibition increased daily and receipts averaged five hundred dollars a day. The name "General Tom Thumb" became a household word, his pictures appeared in all the newspapers and plays, and dances and commodities bore his name. London hostesses vied with one another in having the General appear at their parties, paying him handsomely for this privilege. Many a night he made appearances at two or more parties, very much to his financial gain.

After an extremely successful tour of Great Britain lasting three years, Mr. Barnum and his party moved on to Paris. Once again the little General made a conquest of royalty. King and Queen, prince and princesses, dukes and duchesses were there to view the tiny American who captivated all with his cleverness. At the end of the entertainment, King Louis Philippe presented Tom an emerald brooch set with diamonds and, at the King's request, Mr. Barnum pinned it to Tom Thumb's coat. This was only one of the many priceless gifts lavished upon the General during his Paris visit.

In Paris every performance, afternoon and evening, was sold out. After the evening levee, Tom Thumb appeared in a French play, "Petit Pouce" written expressly for him. Before leaving France, Tom Thumb learned enough French to be able to present the play in the French language, spoken like a native. After leaving Paris, parts of the play were added to the rgeular performances.

The final exhibitions of the tour were given in Dublin. Successful beyond his imagination, Mr. Barnum left Europe highly pleased with the fortune the tour added to his bank account. The entire party set sail for America in February, 1852.

Tom Thumb's success in Europe added greatly to his prestige in his homeland. He resumed exhibitions at Barnum's American Museum and attendance broke all records. Added to his program was his appearance in the little court dress presented him by Queen Victoria. The fact that he had appeared before the Queen and at principal courts of Europe greatly added to his popularity. The presents which had been lavished upon him in Europe were on display in glass cases and provided the basis for one of the General's practical jokes. While

18

TOM THUMB AS NAPOLEON

19

in the middle of one of his numbers he suddenly stopped and shouted, "Mr. Barnum, the case containing my choicest presents has been taken from the table!"

Instantly confusion broke out in the audience. Two men were stationed at the door to prevent escape of the robbers. The General's father immediately offered a reward of $500.00, and Mr. Barnum raced for the police. Just as he was going through the door the General called, "How large is the reward for the person who recovers the jewels?"

"Five hundred dollars," shouted Mr. Barnum.

"Better make it a thousand dollars and make it worth while," called back the General.

"I will," announced Mr. Barnum. "It shall be a thousand."

"Well," said the General, "if you have a thousand to offer, I'll save you the trouble of going for the police."

Whereupon he lifted up the edge of the carpet at the back of the stage where he had secreted the case. He explained that in Belgium the case was stolen and after that the custom of passing it through the audience was discontinued, but back in New York Mr. Barnum had resumed the practice. Tom Thumb thought to give him a lesson he would not forget.

About this time in his career there appeared in a Boston newspaper an account of a trip to New York the General made on the old Fall River line on his way back to the city from New England. Daniel Webster was a fellow passenger. The article was entitled:

THE PIGMY AND THE GIANT

"It was our fortune on Saturday last to take passage for New York on the splendid new steamer, Bay State, which is one of the new line to New York via Fall River. Soon after being on board, we discovered that we had among our fellow travelers two distinguished individuals representing the two extremes of society — the largest man and the smallest one in the country — Daniel Webster and General Tom Thumb. Here in the same cabin was a representative of Brobdignog and Lilliput, and we were the fortunate Gulliver, privileged to see them both at once . . ."

Soon after returning from Europe, Tom Thumb severed his connection with the American Museum. An arrangement was made whereby Mr. Barnum would receive one-half the profits of Tom's tours made on his own, and Mr. Stratton, in Tom's interest, would receive the remaining half of Tom's earnings. Tom Thumb had not only provided Mr. Barnum with a good sized fortune, but had made his parents people of wealth. Upon their return from Europe, Tom's parents built a handsome house in which they lived for the rest of their lives. The house stood until 1953 when it was torn down in the march of progress.

When he spent a vacation in Bridgeport, Tom's neighbors and old friends found him much changed from the little boy who lived among them the first four years of his life. European travel and hobnobbing with kings and queens had turned him into a polished, sophisticated young man. While much of this transformation was due to the sympathetic tutelage of Mr. Barnum, it was equally due to Tom's natural intelligence and his ability to quickly adapt himself to the new circumstances of his life.

At about this time, ill luck began dogging Mr. Barnum's footsteps. He suffered one disaster after another. His businesses failed, he lost the American Museum in New York, and his beautiful home, Iranistan, in Bridgeport, was burned to the ground. Tom Thumb wrote him a letter of condolence and offered to do anything in his power to help. Tom consented to go with Mr. Barnum on another tour of Europe which was so successful that Barnum recouped his fortune and was able to buy back the American Museum. He never ceased to be grateful to Tom Thumb for making all this possible.

After the Museum was again established on a paying basis, Tom continued his travels under his own management. It was while he was away on one of these tours that Barnum introduced to the public another midget. The new attraction was George Washington Morrison Nutt, son of Major Rodnia Nutt of Manchester, New Hampshire. Mr. Barnum instructed one of his New England agents to contact the father and make

COMMODORE NUTT
From a life size painting displayed in the Middleborough Public
Library.

PHINEAS T. BARNUM

Courtesy of Middleborough Historical Museum

If P. T. Barnum's circus was the greatest show on earth, Barnum himself was the greatest showman. It was entirely due to his superlative showmanship that General and Mrs. Tom Thumb became the most famous midgets the world has ever known.

arrangements to exhibit the son. The sum of $30,000 was offered. Thus the new acquisition came to be known as the "Thirty Thousand Dollar Nutt," having been christened by Barnum, "Commodore Nutt."

Barnum achieved another piece of clever showmanship when he added a new vehicle to those in which the little people appeared in parades in the towns and cities where they gave performances. This was a tiny "Walnut Shell Coach," built expressly for Commodore Nutt. The little carriage was shaped like a walnut shell, mounted on wheels, with a high seat in front for the diminutive coachman. Fan shaped windows on either side allowed the occupant to see and be seen. After Tom Thumb married Lavinia and they spent their summers in Middleborough, each year the little walnut coach was refurbished with gilt paint at the carriage paint shop of Admiral J. Bailey. This gave townspeople an opportunity to view the coach and for the children to sit in it.

The Bridgeport Advertiser and Farmer of March 5, 1860, had this to say about General Tom Thumb:

> ". . . The Little General is now twenty-two years old. Of course his age and experience have served to expand his intellect, and he is now not only the smallest, but also the most witty and sagacious traveler to be met with. He is 'not married yet,' all reports to the contrary. The little beau wishes it to be understood that he is still in the matrimonial market, although judging from the numerous and eligible chances he has let slip, he seems rather hard to please . . ."

Unbeknown to Tom, his situation was soon to change; Lavinia Warren, the future Mrs. Tom Thumb, was about to make her appearance at the American Museum.

Chapter II
THE FAIRY WEDDING

Lavinia's appearance at the American Museum was delayed because the jeweler had not completed her jewels. Barnum was prepared to pay her one thousand dollars a week for her appearance, but while awaiting the jewels, Lavinia received an offer to appear before the crowned heads of Europe. She wrote a letter to Barnum telling him she was leaving immediately from Boston and declining his offer to appear at his Museum. Barnum left New York in hot pursuit, traveling by way of Middleborough to persuade Lavinia's parents to accompany him to Boston and use their influence to dissuade their daughter from leaving for Europe — a journey that ended in victory for the showman. A new contract was signed promising that after three or four weeks at the Museum, Lavinia would be free to leave for Europe (with a few extra pounds in her pocket). Thus did Lavinia become one of Barnum's most famous and most profitable attractions.

When General Tom Thumb met Lavinia, it was love at first sight. After meeting her during her stay at the St. Nicholas Hotel, he found excuses to become a daily visitor. He soon sought out his friend and benefactor and declared his intention to marry Lavinia. He believed she was created explicitly to be his wife. He begged his friend to say a good word in his behalf. Barnum said he would do what he could but Tom must do his own courting.

The situation became complicated when Commodore Nutt also fell in love with Lavinia. She had unwittingly encouraged him by presenting him with a ring which did not fit her finger.

The rivalry between the two little men became more and more keen. Every time Tom Thumb came near, the Commodore bristled and attempted to shoo him away. Like two bantam roosters they circled and sidestepped until they finally came to blows. It turned out to be a more or less friendly scuffle and they soon declared a sort of peace.

The General became very impatient. Lavinia did not repulse his attentions, neither did she noticeably encourage him. Tom begged Mr. Barnum to invite Lavinia for a weekend at his home in Bridgeport. He thought this would give him the opportunity to introduce Lavinia to his mother, show her his ponies and carriage and the large amount of real estate he had acquired, all of which he hoped would impress Lavinia with the desirability of becoming his wife.

One Friday morning as Lavinia waited to go on the stage, Mr. Barnum said to her, "Lavinia, I would like you to go home with me to Bridgeport for the rest of the week."

Lavinia accepted with alacrity. Commodore Nutt, overhearing the conversation, said he would also like to go to Bridgeport that weekend to see his ponies which he kept there. Barnum gave his consent but said he would expect the Commodore to give his usual Saturday evening performance at the Museum and catch the late evening train for Bridgeport.

Upon their arrival at Bridgeport, Barnum and Lavinia were met at the station by Tom Thumb with his carriage and coachman. After leaving Mr. Barnum at his home, the two little lovers drove about the city, Tom Thumb making the most of his opportunity to point out all his possessions. A stop was made at his own home where Lavinia was introduced to Mrs. Stratton, who showed Lavinia Tom's own apartment filled with furniture to suit the occupant's diminutive size.

That evening Mrs. Stratton and Tom Thumb dined with Mr. Barnum and his guest. At his own suggestion, the General was invited to remain for the night. As it neared retiring time, the host remarked that someone would have to sit up to greet the Commodore when he arrived on the late evening train. Tom Thumb offered to do so if Lavinia would keep him company.

26

As they waited together, Mr. Barnum having discreetly retired to his chamber, conversation turned to Lavinia's proposed trip to Europe. Tom Thumb asked Lavinia if she were not afraid of being lonesome so far from friends and family. He suggested that he himself could be of great assistance to her since he had already made a tour of Europe. Lavinia agreed that would be very pleasant. Becoming bolder, Tom Thumb ventured, "Don't you think it would be even more pleasant if we went as husband and wife?"

Lavinia pretended to be greatly surprised, but she admitted being favorably disposed.

"However," she said, "I have always said I would never marry without my mother's consent. And that may not be easy to obtain because you know my mother does not approve of you." Mrs. Bump considered Tom Thumb proud, haughty and arrogant, and she disapproved of the mustache he was hopefully cultivating.

Tom Thumb was hastily agreeing to seek the consent of Lavinia's parents when there was a loud stamping on the porch, a sharp ringing of the doorbell and the Commodore had arrived. When he caught sight of his rival he was greatly annoyed, rushed upstairs to Mr. Barnum's room and asked testily, "Does Tom Thumb LIVE here?"

The Commodore retired in a huff to his own room and slammed the door. Just then Tom Thumb came dashing up the stairs and into Mr. Barnum's room announcing gleefully, "She said yes! She said yes! We're engaged!"

Swearing Mr. Barnum to secrecy until they could obtain the mother's consent, Tom went off to bed, a happy little man.

The next day a decision had to be made. Who would break the news to Commodore Nutt? No one wanted to be the one to do it. Finally Lavinia bravely said, "I will tell him myself."

So the news was broken to the Commodore that he had lost the prize. It was a crushing blow, but he found some comfort in the thought that perhaps Lavinia's mother would not give her consent.

Tom Thumb decided the best way to present his case to Mrs. Bump was by letter to be delivered by a personal friend.

27

This friend, George A. Wells, traveled to Middleborough bearing, besides a letter from Tom Thumb, one from Lavinia urging her mother to put aside her prejudices and consent to the marriage. At first Mrs. Bump demurred, fearing the wedding was but another of Barnum's schemes for publicity, but after reading Lavinia's letter she was convinced it was definitely a case of love. Upon being assured by Mr. Wells that to prove his good faith, Barnum was willing to cancel Lavinia's contract, Mrs. Bump gave her blessing.

The announcement of the engagement caused great excitement and a tremendous increase in attendance at the Museum. Ever since her debut, Lavinia had sold a little card bearing her photograph. Now Tom Thumb's picture was added and hundreds of these souvenirs were sold every day. The wedding date was set, February 10, 1863. Mr. Barnum was not slow in telling the world about it. So great was the sensation caused by word of the approaching marriage that news of the Civil War was forced off the front pages of newspapers.

A fortune was pouring in to the coffers at the Museum and Barnum was loathe to have this bonanza come to an end. He offered the happy couple fifteen thousand dollars if they would postpone the wedding for a month, but both parties were adamant in their refusal.

"Not for fifty thousand dollars," firmly said the General.

"Not for one hundred thousand," said Lavinia.

Mr. Barnum was then tempted with visions of the fortune that could be made by having the wedding in the Museum and charging admission, but he put this temptation behind him by reminding himself he had promised to give his proteges a dignified wedding.

To the impatient bridegroom February tenth was long in arriving. A suggestion was made that Valentine's Day would be an appropriate date, but Tom would not even consider it. The chosen place was Grace Church in New York City, the time high noon. Long before that hour the area about the church was thronged with people eager for a glimpse of this most unusual wedding party.

Admittance to the church was by card. These prettily decorated bits of cardboard were avidly sought and fabulous sums were offered for them. Mr. Barnum stifled whatever temptation he may have had to capitalize on the event by charging admission and distributed the cards among the elite and celebrities of the hour. These included President and Mrs. Lincoln, members of the President's Cabinet, diplomats of this country and abroad, not forgetting officers of the United States Army who had distinguished themselves on the field of battle of the Civil War then in progress.

THE FAIRY WEDDING
Grace Church, New York City
February 10, 1863

Because the usual steps to the chancel were far too high to be negotiated gracefully by four such tiny people, a low platform was constructed for the occasion with six shallow steps leading to the alter, carpeted like the aisle of the church. Admittance cards requested that dress be formal, and it was indeed a gay and richly attired assemblage that awaited the arrival of the bridal party. With a bustle and stir the first of the clergy arrived.

Each of the bridal couple was represented by a minister from their own church. The Reverend Junius Willey of St. John's Church of Bridgeport, Connecticut, assisted the Reverend Thomas H. Taylor, D.D., Rector of Grace Church, who officiated at the ceremony. The Reverend Israel W. Putnam, D.D., of the

29

First Congregational Church of Middleborough, Massachusetts, pastor and close friend of the bride and her family, gave the bride in marriage.

The clergy took their seats within the chancel and the familiar strains of the wedding march filled the church. The audience stood, some on tiptoe, some on the seats of the pews the better to see the tiniest of all wedding parties as it proceeded down the aisle. The procession was led by Mr. Barnum who towered high above the bridal group. Following him was Commodore Nutt and on his arm the tiny bridesmaid, Minnie Warren, younger sister of the bride, even more petite than the bride herself. Because of his disappointment and pique at having lost Lavinia to his rival, the Commodore at first refused to take any part in the wedding, but after much persuasian he reluctantly consented to serve as best man.

The two attendants were followed closely by General Tom Thumb and Lavinia, the bride radiant in her happiness. The four tiny principals took their places before the chancel and the Reverend Willey arose to begin the ceremony. The response of the bride and groom were given in firm, distinct tones, heard clearly throughout the church.

The bride's wedding gown was an exquisite creation of white satin and lace, fashioned with a flowing train and decorated with beads and pearls. Her hair was arranged a la Eugenie, and the bridal veil, caught by two diamond stars, was held in place by a crown of orange blossoms. Her little white kid gloves measured from wrist to tip of middle finger only four and one-half inches, the finger but one and one-half inches long. White satin slippers with rosettes of lace and pearls and a point lace handkerchief not much larger than a postage stamp completed the bride's costume.

The bridal bouquet was of roses and japonicas, fashioned in the shape of a star. The jewels adorning the bride were a gift from the groom, all of dazzling diamonds consisting of a necklace with sparkling pendants, bracelets set with diamond stars, a brooch in the form of an eight-pointed star with earrings to match, and the two diamond stars for her veil.

THE GENERAL AND HIS BRIDE

General Tom Thumb was arrayed for his wedding in a full dress suit, white corded silk vest, blue silk undervest, white gloves, and shining black boots. The Commodore was similarly attired, his undervest of pink silk.

Minnie Warren, the diminutive bridesmaid, was just fourteen years old, and less than a yard high. While Lavinia's face was round and full, Minnie's was heart-shaped, lending a most winsome expression to her countenance. She was captivating in a white dress of silk adorned with tulle puffings and pink rosebuds with a matching wreath of rosebuds in her hair.

The ceremony completed, the fairy-like wedding party came down the aisle and entered their carriages, driven through cheering crowds to the Metropolitan Hotel where a reception was held for ten thousand guests. The petite quartet was lifted onto a grand piano and from there greeted their guests to avoid being crushed by the throng of people. On the right of the groom stood Commodore Nutt and on the left of the bride, Minnie Warren. In the minds of many of those present was the thought that in all probability there would soon be another fairy wedding with these two as principals, but that was never to be. Commodore Nutt never married.

For the reception the bride was gowned in changeable taffeta, shading from pale amber to white. On each panel was embroidered emblems of the nations: a rose for England, laurel for France, an acorn with oak leaves for Germany, a shamrock for Ireland, a thistle for Scotland, grapes on the vine for Italy, and growing corn for America. These designs were fashioned of narrow folds of white satin and each panel was separated by Marabout feathers and lace. The sides of the skirt were looped high over an underskirt of white silk trimmed with seed pearls and puffings of tulle. The bodice was ornamented with narrow folds of white satin and lace. Mr. Barnum ordered the gown to be made by Madame Demorest of Broadway, New York City, who was instructed to spare no expense.

The hundreds of wedding gifts were displayed in glass cases and are too numerous to mention in detail, but included among the most interesting were:

A diamond studded watch, enclosed within two enameled grape leaves, each decorated with a cluster of diamond grapes that parted to reveal the dial, accompanied by a matching chatelaine pin, a gift of Ball, Black & Company.

THE WEDDING PARTY AT RECEPTION
Receiving their guests atop a grand piano to avoid being crushed
by the throng.

A small billiard table, three feet by six, elaborately carved and inlaid with small diamond shaped pieces of ivory, with balls, cues and rack to match, a gift of Phelan & Callender.

A miniature silver horse and chariot, eyes of the horse being garnets and the chariot ornamented with rubies, a gift of Tiffany & Company.

A set of gold charms, wrought in the form of cupid's bow and quiver, cap of Liberty, and watch key, all of the tiniest size, to be worn on the bride's dainty wrist, a gift of August Belmont, Esq.

A small rosewood chair, twelve inches in height, richly carved and upholstered in blue velvet, a gift of M. G. Herter.

A miniature sewing machine, twenty-six inches in height and twenty-one inches long, silver plated with a rosewood case, gift of Wheeler & Wilson Company.

A miniature set of parlor furniture, ebony and gold, a gift of Mrs. George A. Wells.

A Chinese firescreen of gold, silver and pearl, a gift of Mrs. Abraham Lincoln.

A tortoise shell case from which arose a beautiful bird in natural feathers which, with a shake of its brilliant plumage, burst into song. A gift of P. T. Barnum.

After viewing the gifts and partaking of refreshments, each guest was given a piece of the wedding cake, which was an elaborate affair weighing eighty pounds and ornamented with an intricate leaf and shell design with cupids scattering flowers from horns of plenty. The whole was surmounted with a replica of an Egyptian Temple of Fame, the columns bearing cupids and angels. Beneath the arches of the temple stood a replica of the bride and groom taking the matrimonial vows before a tiny minister in clerical robes. On the extreme top of the temple was the Angel of Fame proclaiming to the world the joyous tidings that General Tom Thumb and Lavinia Warren were now man and wife.

The cake was distributed among the guests, each piece encased in a tiny white box. Pieces of this cake are still treasured by families of the recipients. One box is in a glass case at the Middleborough Historical Museum, presented by Theodore N. Wood, whose father attended the ceremony. The box has never been opened.

GENERAL AND MRS. TOM THUMB
Soon after their marriage

At ten o'clock in the evening, the New York Excelsior Band serenaded the bridal couple while throngs of people stood in the streets. The General appeared on the balcony and addressed the crowd, concluding his speech with the words, "I will make this speech, like myself, short." New York newspapers made the most of so extraordinary an event and accounts of the wedding were spread upon the front pages of every newspaper.

After a day crowded with excitement, the General and his wife left on their bridal tour. The first stop was Philadelphia, where a reception awaited them at the Continental Hotel. From Philadelphia, they went on to Baltimore and Washington. Here they were received by President and Mrs. Lincoln who gave a reception in honor of the newly-weds. The President observed that General Tom Thumb and his bride, not the President of the United States, were the center of attention that evening.

Following their honeymoon tour, the couple retired to Lavinia's home in Middleborough for a rest. While there, a representative of the local paper, the Middleboro Gazette, interviewed the bridal pair and an account of the visit was published in the issue of March 21, 1863:

"These petite celebrities, about whose bridal ceremonies such eclat was raised in New York, have been sojourning for a week or two at the residence of the bride's parents in Middleboro . . . The parents of the bride are plain, sensible people of well-developed and robust physique, and with their tall and well proportioned older daughter, form a singular contrast to the elfin fairies, Lavinia and Minnie. The General and his Lady are sociable, sprightly and communicative, perfectly self-possessed and at ease in their new relations and apparently as happy as any young couple on their bridal tour.

Through the courtesy of the sister, Mrs. Southworth, and Madame Letaire, their lady traveling companion who formerly accompanied Jenny Lind in the same relation, we were privileged with a full display of the wardrobe, bridal presents, et cetera . . .

From the white satin wedding dress with lace overskirt, through the whole eighteen to the maize-colored Victoria presentation dress, with skirt looped to the waist, and satin underskirt embroidered with a thousand pearls in various figures, all was in the highest style and finish — blue, crimson, salmon, straw, white, green, orange silks and satins, plain, figured, and embroidered with raised velvet figures.

Mrs. Editor was enthusiastic in admiration of the "small wares" from which we refrained our sacreligous gaze. She mentions hoop skirts covered with silk, tiny white satin quilted corsets, manufactured by the General's brother-in-law, Bassett & Co., tiny gloves, satin slippers and lace bridal veil which alone cost $190, and other expensive articles of delicate and gossamer texture. The gallant General displayed his gift to the bride, a set of jewelry, consisting of necklace, hairpins, and bracelets, costing five thousand dollars. The General assisted us to solve the mathematical problem as to the number of diamonds, which proved to be two hundred and fifty six . . . Then catching the hand of his little bride, he naively remarked, "Here is the engagement ring," as he held it up, showing a glistening diamond ten fold the size of either kunckle around it. There was a set of costly white ermine, cape, muff and muftees, presented by C. C. Gunther of New York, and a miniature gold watch encased in a gold leaf less than an inch long. The dial of the watch was half an inch in diameter with hour, minute and second hand; these, with a number of other costly gifts consisting of albums, writing cases, silverware and jewelry, attracted notice and explanation as to donors, until our lengthy stay had outraged our sense of propriety, and we left with the compliments of the world renowned couple, photographs, cards and cake, gracefully presented by the bride.

As we passed the window, the General encircled his arm around the neck of his sweet little bit of humanity and imprinted an affectionate salute on her blushing cheek. Quick as a flash she raised the window and coquettishly called out to us, 'Don't you put THAT in the paper,' to which, of course, we agreed."

MARRIAGE CEREMONY AT GRACE CHURCH, FEBRUARY 10, 1863.

The marriage as pictured in booklet published by Wynkoop and Hallenbeck of New York City in 1867.

Chapter III
THE WIDE, WIDE WORLD

After their honeymoon, General and Mrs. Tom Thumb took a brief rest from public appearances and then embarked upon a life of travel that was to take them all over their own country and to the far corners of the earth.

Mr. Barnum had made plans for a European trip to begin in October, 1863. Sylvester Bleeker was engaged to arrange an entertainment that would include, in addition to the General and his wife, her sister Minnie and Commodore Nutt, the midget Barnum had discovered in Manchester, New Hampshire. The sketches and short plays enacted by the four little people proved so successful that Barnum requested them to fill in the time until October by making a tour of New England and Canada. Leaving New York, the group were passengers on the last train to run on tracks torn up the following morning because of Civil War riots.

Mr. Bleeker and his little company visited cities in Connecticut and continued on to Worcester, Massachusetts, and to Boston, where entertainments were given in Tremont Temple. The next destination was Canada. By the time they visited Montreal, Toronto, and other cities in the Dominion, it was October and time to leave on their European journey. However, Mr. Bleeker realized that a great deal of money could be made by continuing this tour and he wrote to Mr. Barnum urging a postponement of the European trip, remarking that to leave then would be throwing away the cream. Quickly came the reply from Barnum, "By all means save the cream."

The group returned to the United States, going into the Southern states. Everywhere they had to contend with conditions made difficult by the War. In Wheeling, Virginia, the hotel was crowded with soldiers. They monopolized the dining room, the waiters and the food. Losing his patience, Commodore Nutt rushed into the kitchen, laid hands on a huge platter of ham and staggered back to the dining room. Several soldiers standing nearby sprang to his assistance and, assuming the role of waiters, transferred many delicacies from their own table to that of the little folk.

Mrs. Tom Thumb, who loved excitement, persuaded Mr. Bleeker to go into Kentucky. Wilkes Booth was playing in a theatre in Louisville and his hotel room was opposite that of the Tom Thumbs. He gave his picture to Mrs. Tom Thumb and she had it with her in London when word reached them of the assassination of President Lincoln. As they continued their trip into the deep south, their route several times crossed the fighting lines. After reaching Tennessee they deemed it prudent to return home. They had been away from New York eleven months and, although they charged only twenty-five cents admission for adults and fifteen cents for children, the trip netted a tidy profit of $12,000 — pure cream indeed.

At long last, the company was ready for their trip to Europe. They set sail from New York on October 29, 1865, landing at Liverpool, where they were greeted by a huge gathering curious to catch a glimpse of these famous little people from America. Later, throngs gathered every time the Tom Thumbs appeared in their little coach drawn by Shetland ponies as they were transported to the hall where their entertainment was to take place. This brought traffic to a standstill. In fact, the General several times was arrested for obstructing traffic, but was always rescued by his lawyer. Tom Thumb found this all very amusing and admitted to driving about the streets more than was necessary, just to enjoy the confusion of the bobbies.

The Sunday following their arrival in Liverpool was Mayor's Day and the General's party stepped out onto the hotel balcony to view the parade. The crowd solidified in front of the balcony, shouting and cheering not the Mayor, but the four little

The tiny coach and Shetland ponies used by the Tom Thumbs in parades before each performance, later used by Count and Countess Magri and Baron Magri.

Americans on the balcony. Whenever the midgets appeared on the streets great crowds followed them, making sightseeing for them impossible. Because of the crush of people that gathered the minute they ventured out of their hotel room, the four little people were forced to remain in their rooms. They learned to while away the long hours by doing needlework, the men as well as the women becoming adept in executing large pieces, chiefly of needlepoint.

Visits were made to London and Paris. In June, 1865, Tom Thumb made another appearance before Queen Victoria, this time with his tiny bride. The General and the Queen laughed together over memories of his previous visit when the Queen's little spaniel upset the decorum of the meeting. After this royal visit, all printed programs and brochures about the levees of the Tom Thumb troupe were headed with the Royal Court of Arms, a privilege accorded to those who had been favored by her Majesty Queen Victoria.

The visit in Great Britain lasted more than a year, followed by a tour of Ireland and Wales. On June 12, 1866, the General and his entire party set sail from Liverpool to America. Upon their arrival, General and Mrs. Tom Thumb went immediately to their home in Middleborough for a complete rest. After this brief respite, the troupe set out again to cover

THE WALNUT SHELL COACH
Built expressly for Commodore Nutt

ONE OF THE TOM THUMB COACHES

that part of the south that the Civil War prevented them visiting on the previous tour. Their travels concluded in San Antonio, Texas, where they met with unexpected success, profits reaching one thousand dollars a week.

At this point of the tour, Mr. Bleeker received a letter from Mr. Barnum that was to send them all on a journey to lands none of them ever expected to visit. The letter exploded like a bomb shell. In part it read, "An idea has occurred to me in which I can see a 'Golden Gate' opening for the General Tom Thumb Company. What do you think of a 'Tour Around the World,' including Australia? Decide quickly. If you consent to undertake the journey, prepare to start next month."

Each one of the company could think of any number of reasons why the trip should not be made. It was the thought of going to the unknown land of Australia that frightened them all. After a long discussion, an article of agreement was drawn up whereby all countries mentioned, except Australia, should be visited. If the manager, Mr. Bleeker, deemed it best from a financial standpoint to visit Australia, the objection of the little folk would be waived and that country included in the itinerary.

A short vacation of two weeks was taken to replenish wardrobes and bid farewell to families and friends. On June 12, 1869, the momentous journey was begun. The party consisted of the four midgets, Mr. and Mrs. Bleeker, a treasurer, agent, general assistant and doorkeeper, a pianist, the groom Rodnia Nutt, Jr., the little coach and four of the smallest ponies available. Throughout the long journey the stamina and endurance of the four tiny principals of the company were amazing, far in excess of their diminutive size. They never faltered or complained when time and again the rest of the party was ready to give up.

The journey to the west coast was made overland. From the start a daily schedule was set of one hundred and ten miles of travel and two performances. Towns which today are flourishing and thickly settled, then consisted of a canvas railroad station and a few adobe houses. Part of the way was traveled by train and passengers on the Union Pacific were in great fear of attacking Indians. There were no incidents, although many Indians were sighted along the route.

A closer contact was made at Corinne, Utah. Indians were everywhere. Word of the little visitors reached the Indian camp outside of town. A contingent of Indians galloped into town and gathered before the hotel. When it was time to depart for the performance and the ponies and little coach drew up before the hotel, the four small performers entered the coach and left for the place of entertainment. They were followed by a shouting, yelling mob of Indians, but only the leader was allowed inside the hall to witness the performance.

Travel between towns was beset with many dangers. On one occasion, only by avoiding the regular stagecoach and chartering a coach that left several hours in advance, did the company avert a holdup by brigands. The regular coach was held up in a mountain pass, but the Tom Thumb troupe had already reached their destination. The ride down the mountain, however, had its own hazards. The narrow road was cut into the side of the mountain. The horses wore leather shields to protect their sides as they hugged the inside of the road. The driver left it all to the horses. At the beginning of the descent, he whipped up the animals to a fast trot that was maintained all the way down the steep grade, the carriage rocking and reeling behind, until the bottom of the trail was reached.

On August 2, 1869, the party arrived in San Francisco where they received a great ovation. Three levees a day were held for two weeks and streets leading to the hall were thronged with people waiting to see the little folk ride to and from the hotel in their tiny coach.

Although the party was to sail for Japan from San Francisco, Mr. Bleeker was eager to take the company to Oregon. This meant more dangerous traveling. Two coaches with two expert drivers and eight horses were hired to make the journey over mountain and plain. Once the party became lost on the plain; on another occasion Mrs. Bleeker, Lavinia and Minnie were nearly killed when the horses ran away while the menfolk were inquiring about directions at a roadside inn. Because of the steep mountains to be crossed, very often everyone would alight from the coaches and walk, even the four small passengers, trudging three and four miles to relieve the horses. Arriving in some isolated town, a performance would be given attended by crowds who had come from miles around and waited for hours to see these famous little people. The program was presented with verve and spirit, the audiences never suspecting how weary were the small performers.

Proceeding over mountains infested with bears and often covered with deep snow, stopping at toll houses, cabins, wherever they could find a night's lodging, the party finally arrived in Oregon. After appearing before large audiences in Oregon City, Salem, and Portland, the return was made to San Francisco by boat. On November 4, 1869, the entire group set sail on the Pacific mail steamer, "American," for Yokohama, Japan.

After a stormy voyage, the ship arrived in Yokohama Harbor on the last day of November. As the retinue of Americans passed along the streets they were followed by a great crowd of curious Japanese, hundreds dashing out from alleys and shops to join the throng. The Japanese women could not resist touching the two little ladies and would repeat, "Mellican?, Mellican?"

Some of the Japanese customs shocked the American visitors. Tom Thumb had heard of the custom of common bathing for men, women, and children, but said he could not believe it until he had seen it. One morning Mr. Bleeker and Tom paid a visit to one of the large bath houses. They were confronted by two women with elaborate hairdress and costumes who served as ticket sellers. When they observed the tiny General they began to giggle. Tom was so short he could not see the bathers, so he and Mr. Bleeker were given permission to go inside, and in a moment the two Americans stood where few foreigners had ever been allowed to go. In a tank about twenty feet square were fourteen people including men, women, boys and little girls. Some were vigorously scrubbing, the boys were wrestling, and the little girls were splashing each other. As Mr. Bleeker and Tom turned to go, the bathers caught sight of them and all rushed from the bath and crowded around to get a better view of Tom Thumb. The embarrassed pair beat a hasty retreat and once outside, walked some distance in silence, broken at last by Tom Thumb who remarked, "If P. T. Barnum had that place in the United States it would be the biggest show he ever had."

The troupe visited Nagasaki, little suspecting that one day the small town would hold a place in history. They sailed across the Yellow Sea to China, landing near Shanghai. The ponies drew the little coach through crowded streets followed by Chinamen carrying handsome silken banners advertising the performance for that evening. To set the stage for each levee, the ponies and coach with coachman Rodnia Nutt, Jr., holding the reins, were placed at the back of the stage. As the four little performers advanced on the stage, they were greeted by applause followed by murmers of wonder and admiration.

The four midgets went through their act: Lavinia sang, Commodore Nutt danced and acted the comedian, General Tom Thumb presented impersonations in costume, and all four joined in a pantomime play. At the close of the program a five year old Chinese boy with a long pigtail was lifted up onto the stage, and, hand in hand, he and Minnie, of equal size, strutted about the stage, to the great delight of the audience.

After visiting other Chinese cities, the group set sail on December 28, 1869, for the next port of call, Singapore, India. Here they met the Maharajah and had the unusual privilege of visiting the women's quarters, so curious were the Ranee and her attendants to meet Tom Thumb and the other little Americans. The Americans were charmed with the Ranee and the little princess who had fourteen attendants, one for each year of her age. Members of the royal family were lavishly attired in robes of rich silks and ablaze with diamonds, but all were with bare feet.

During the visit to Indian cities and their hotels, the Americans encountered some puzzling customs. The native servants seemed unable to recognize linens of various uses, and sheets were found on dining tables, tablecloths on the beds, and pillow cases on the towel racks. Sanitation practices were questionable and the party ate from dishes that were best not too closely inspected.

Colombo and Ceylon were among two places visited. Travel was hazardous between these points, made by two coaches each drawn by four horses. Part of the region contained gold fields, and Lavinia purchased for Minnie a bracelet made of native gold, engraved with the date, June 2, 1870, and an inscription. The bracelet was so poignant a reminder of her sister and their happy days together that after Minnie's death, it became one of Lavinia's most treasured possessions and she was seldom without it.

Plans were now made to continue the tour of Victoria and on to South Australia. On the Isle of Tasmania, stops were made at all accessible towns. Often there were not suitable accommodations for living or for their performances, but they all made the best of what was available. In Oatlands, a stable and coach house were cleared and used, the grain room serving as a dressing room. One inn keeper, wishing to do something special for his guests, announced he would serve them an American supper. His guests looked forward to the meal with keen anticipation, but when they sat down at the table they were confronted with dishes of boiled pumpkin and salt pork!

The passage to South Australia was very rough and the ship was given up for lost. After landing safely, plans were made to cross the sandy desert. Mr. Bleeker was strongly advised not to make the trip with the coaches. Travel would be not only slow but very dangerous. The horses would be up to their middle in sand and provisions for both humans and animals would have to be carried, as on the desert there were only bark sheds at intervals of twenty miles.

Mr. Bleeker weighed the matter carefully. Charges would be tremendous to carry the party and coaches by steamer and it was necessary to have the coaches for use in Australia. He made up his mind the results would be worth the risks, and knew that whatever his decision, his little company would follow. Before the trip was ended, he was to have many misgivings about the wisdom of his decision.

Fearing the small ponies would not be equal to the journey across the desert, these and the little coach were sent by steamer. All the dire predictions proved true. The horses were above their knees in sand, and to save them the party walked two-thirds of the time, sinking deep in sand with every step. Sometimes their only guide in the wastes of sand were tracks of a mail coach which had crossed two days ahead of them.

Mr. Bleeker suffered a harrowing experience. Walking faster than the others, he was far in advance of them. After some time, he realized he was following a wheel track which circled a hill and was not the one made by the mail coach. He waited some time, but when the coaches did not appear, decided to press on two miles by the present route and if by that time the rest of the party had not put in an appearance, to retrace his steps to the small station where they had spent the night. As he plodded along he heard loud screams over his head and looking up, saw an enormous eagle circling above him. Knowing an Australian eagle will not hesitate to attack a human being or an object as large as a full grown kangaroo, Mr. Bleeker was badly frightened, aware there was not stick nor stone with which to defend himself. Standing perfectly still, he hoped the bird would lose interest and fly away.

Each circle brought the eagle closer to its victim until at last it made a final swoop. At the same instant Mr. Bleeker dropped to the earth and the eagle swept over him so close its wings brushed his body. Jumping to his feet, Mr. Bleeker ran. The air was rent by the bird's screams and the circles increased in speed. This continued about a mile, the eagle occasionally positioning itself for a dip downward, but instead darting off ahead. After what seemed an interminable distance, the eagle suddenly changed its course and sailed away out of sight. The natives told Mr. Bleeker it was his running that saved his life. Had he stopped, the big bird would have undoubtedly attacked and killed him.

The track in the sand continued on and Mr. Bleeker was fast becoming convinced he had taken the wrong turn when suddenly the track veered sharply to the left and led to another which seemed likely to be the one taken by the mail coach. After a discouraging half hour, there came the welcome sound of the drivers' voices shouting to the horses and in a few moments they appeared, with the three ladies plodding along through the sand.

All the passengers continued walking to save the horses, but neither Lavinia nor Minnie would admit to being tired. Each time they were asked, they replied emphatically, "No! We like it!" Food was carried in the coaches and at meal time search was made for fresh water to be found in holes dug in the sand by cattlemen taking their herds across the desert to market. Making about thirty miles a day, they arrived at last at the banks of the Murray River, where they were ferried across to Wellington.

After giving ten performances in towns between Wellington and Adelaide, the party set forth on another hazardous journey. A wide, deep and dangerous river must be forded, a river angry and swollen from recent rains. The driver of one of the coaches looked at the river thoughtfully, then plunged in on one of the more powerful horses. Turning downstream, he disappeared under overhanging trees, then struck diagonally across. The horse sank as if it had stepped off a ledge, then began to swim. Turning, it gained a footing and scrambled up the opposite bank.

The ladies looked pale and anxious but were determined to proceed. Deeper and deeper into the water they went until the horses were entirely submerged with only their heads above water. Inside the coach, water was level with the seats and the passengers sat with their knees drawn up to their chins. The driver, losing courage, pulled up the horses. "Don't stop or you are lost," shouted the guide. The driver applied his whip, the horses lunged forward, but half swimming as they were, they scarcely had strength to move the coach. With a tremendous surge, the horses plunged up the bank. The guide then explained their narrow escape. There were two white crosses, one on each side of the river. A narrow sandbar extended across the river with deep water on either side. A perfectly straight line must be kept between the white crosses or the vehicle would roll off the edge of the bar into the deep, boiling water. So skillful was the guide in following that narrow line, that when the horses climbed the bank, they were beside the white cross.

The goal was now Sidney, and after visiting several towns north of that city, the troupe traveled to Madras, India, having completed a stay in Australia of eight and one-half months. They proceeded to Calcutta and Bombay. En route to Arabia, stops were made in many cities. Continuing toward Suez, their course lay through the Straits of Babel Mandeb into the Red Sea and thence to Suez. They took time to visit Cairo and the Pyramids, after which passage was taken for Europe, arriving at Brindisi, Italy, on March 14, 1871.

After spending approximately a month in Italy, the party embarked for England and the last leg of their long journey, arriving in New York on June 22, 1871. The Tom Thumb Company had circled the world, traveled 55,487 miles and given 1,471 performances, not missing a single engagement because of illness or accident. The trip netted a profit of $80,000.

GENERAL TOM THUMB AND LAVINIA

Chapter IV
TWILIGHT YEARS

After a much needed rest, the now famous quartet resumed their travels, setting out on a tour that took them to every state in the Union. This period of their lives was the most prosperous, and it was at this time that the General and his wife built their home in the Warrentown section of Middleborough, across the road from Lavinia's old home where her family still lived. Everything in the house was built to scale to accommodate its tiny occupants: windows with sills a few inches from the floor and low enough to enable them to look across to Lavinia's old home or to the little red house that was Lavinia's birthplace, also just across the road; stair treads of a height easily managed by a husband and wife no larger than a four-year-old. In the rooms were placed the many pieces of miniature-sized furniture presented by royalty and friends the world over. In the living room was a little set of parlor furniture upholstered in red velvet, the tiny sewing machine that had been a wedding gift, the miniature grand piano presented by Queen Victoria, a wee rocking chair for Lavinia and an equally tiny Morris chair for Tom Thumb. In the bedroom stood the small brass bed with a canopy topped by a crown and in another a carved mahogany bed, a gift of Mr. Barnum. There were tall glass cabinets containing gifts of china and glass and small treasures. The kitchen was equipped with a small, low sink, a small cookstove, and cupboards low enough to be easily reached by a cook only thirty-six inches tall. In the basement a little stove was built into the brick chimney and this small relic remained several years after the house was sold.

51

The home built for General and Mrs. Tom Thumb with the interior constructed to accommodate their miniature size.

It is said that Mr. Stratton, Tom Thumb's father, supervised the building of the house while the little folk were on a tour. Soon after the structure was begun a storm of almost hurricane force completely demolished it. Mr. Stratton sent word of the disaster to his son, asking what to do next. Back came the answer, "Put it up again," which was done.

In the Middleboro Gazette of January 21, 1910, appeared this advertisement:

For sale. Tom Thumb property at Warrentown, consisting of house and stable and two acres of land. Near electric cars. Price $2,400.

Since then the property has had more than one owner. The exterior remains much as it was originally, but gone are the little stairs, the low windows, the tiny sink and cupboards.

While living in this house, Tom Thumb indulged in some of his extravagant pleasures. In the barn were fast horses and smart traps seen often with Tom Thumb holding the reins while enjoying a fast trot on the country roads. He also purchased a yacht. There is a very faded photograph, so indistinct the outline of a yacht can barely be discerned, but on the back of the picture is written, "Tom Thumb's yacht, Maggie Bee." The yacht was kept at Onset, near Buzzards Bay.

At this time, about 1880, the Tom Thumbs owned a small red cottage at Green Point, on Lake Assawampsett, Lakeville, about four miles from Middleborough. Both little people were frequent passengers on the old side-wheeler, "Assawampsett," a steamboat owned and operated by John B. LeBaron of Middleborough. Excursions were conducted from a bridge on Wareham Street in Middleborough up the Nemasket River to Lake Assawampsett and then around the lake, ending at a pavilion at Nelson's Grove where clambakes, picnics, and dancing were enjoyed.

It seems that Tom Thumb may have disposed of his yacht and purchased a catboat to use on the lake. In the "Fifty Years Ago" column in the Middleboro Gazette, August 7, 1931, there appeared this interesting item: "Tom Thumb has exchanged his yacht for a $3,000 diamond ring." It is well known that Tom Thumb owned a catboat and that on the deck was a little brass cannon with which he delighted in saluting the steamer "Assawampsett" as it emerged from the river onto the lake. One day a sudden squall swept the lake overturning many craft, including that of Tom Thumb. The old captain hired by Tom to sail the boat was questioned about the incident and said, "Hm! Nothing to worry about. Tom Thumb came up and sat on a lily pad until he was rescued." The boat was salvaged but, as far as is known, the little brass cannon sank to the bottom of the lake.

Although Mr. Barnum resigned his interest in the company, General Tom Thumb and his wife continued on close friendly terms with their old friend and benefactor, and in 1881 he persuaded the couple to travel with his "Greatest Show on Earth."

On January 10, 1883, the troupe was in Milwaukee, Wisconsin, quartered at the Newhall House. In the middle of the night flames raced through the hotel and the guests were rescued with difficulty. Mrs. Bleeker was so badly injured she died twelve days later. Tom Thumb never recovered from the shock of this terrible experience and died at the home in Mid-

The monument at Tom Thumb's grave
Mountain Grove Cemetery
Bridgeport, Conn.

dleborough the following July. He was taken to Bridgeport, Connecticut, and burial was in Mountain Grove Cemetery.

The married life of Charles Stratton and Lavinia Warren was an unusually happy one. They shared many of the same interests and were of congenial dispositions. Despite the many statements in print and photographs of Lavinia holding a small baby in her arms, no children were ever born to the couple. The photographs of Lavinia and the baby were just another of Barnum's schemes to fool the public; the baby was a borrowed one.

The death of General Tom Thumb was the second break in the ranks of the quartet. Five years previously, on July 23, 1878, Lavinia's beloved sister Minnie died in childbirth at the family home in Middleborough. Minnie was always a shy person, somewhat overshadowed by her vivacious sister Lavinia. She never attained Lavinia's height, never measuring more than thirty-two inches. After returning from their world tour, in the year 1877 at Lock Haven, Pennsylvania, Minnie married another midget, an Englishman, Major Edward Newell. Soon the neighbors saw Minnie making baby clothes — using

54

a doll's pattern. Having been born a doll, she expected a doll-sized baby. But Minnie gave birth to a normal-sized baby weighing close to six pounds. It was a difficult birth and Minnie died from exhaustion; the baby died four hours later.

In her suffering, Minnie begged her sister Lavinia to rock her. After her death, a song was published, written by Horatio C. King, entitled "Rock Me, Sister," a song filled with emotion telling of Minnie Warren's brief and pathetic career.

COMMODORE NUTT AND MINNIE WARREN

GENERAL AND MRS. TOM THUMB
AND BORROWED BABY

No children were born to General and Mrs. Tom Thumb. This picture, circulated widely, was just another of Barnum's schemes to fool the public. The baby was a borrowed one. In a nationally circulated magazine in 1944, appeared this picture with the statement:

"General and Mrs. Tom Thumb and their daughter who was born on December 5, 1863. Harper's Weekly called the baby an 'interesting Thumbling.' The little girl weighed 3 lbs. at birth, only 7¾ lbs. in weight at the age of one year when she was taken on an exhibition tour of Europe. She died in New York City when 2½ years old."

THE ABOVE STATEMENT IS ENTIRELY FALSE.

(see picture, page 56)

Minnie and her baby were buried together at Nemasket Hill Cemetery in Middleborough, in the family plot. A newspaper clipping of the period relates that as they lay together in the tiny white casket, they looked like a little girl with her doll. The small grave is outlined with a granite curbing that indicates how tiny was the casket that held this small mother and her baby.

It was very difficult for Lavinia to appear before the public without her sister Minnie, and after the death of General Tom Thumb she expressed a desire to retire from public life. Mr. Barnum advised her that to retire would only make her more unhappy and lonely, possibly to the extent of shortening her life. Lavinia accepted this advice and continued to fulfill engagements.

HULDAH PIERCE BUMP
"Minnie Warren"

58

BARON MAGRI   COUNT MAGRI
COUNTESS MAGRI

Part of the company was composed of two little midgets, Count Primo and Baron Ernest Magri. The brothers were born in Bologna, Italy, and had eleven brothers and sisters, all normal except Primo, Ernest, and one sister Amalia who died when she was thirty-four years old. The sister was the tallest of the three, a few inches taller than Primo, who was thirty-seven inches tall, and Ernest, who was thirty-eight and one-half inches tall. During their tour of the principal cities of Italy, they were granted an audience by Pope Pius IX who was so delighted with the diminutive pair that he conferred upon them the titles of "Count Primo Magri" and "Baron Ernest Magri." In 1881, their travels took the two little Italians to Australia and New Zealand. It was on their return from this tour that they were engaged to appear on the Barnum circuit with General Tom Thumb and Company. After Tom Thumb's death in 1883, the Count and Baron formed a company with Mrs. Tom Thumb, the two brothers being known for a time as Count Rosebud and Baron Littlefinger.

The friendship between the Count and Lavinia ripened into love, culminating in their marriage on Easter Monday, April 6, 1885, at the Church of the Holy Trinity, New York City. Major Edward Newell, widower of Minnie Warren, served as best man and Miss Sarah Adams, a midget from Oak Bluffs, Massachusetts, and a close friend of Lavinia, was her bridesmaid.

Three thousand guests attended the ceremony. Following is an account of the wedding as presented in a booklet, "Life and Travels of Mrs. General Tom Thumb (Countess Magri) and Biographical Sketch of Count and Baron Magri:"

LITTLE WIDOW THUMB'S WEDDING

At the Church of Holy Trinity, three thousand spectators all stood up together as the bridal party slowly entered. The midget Count Magri with his bride on his arm, looked like elegantly dressed dolls. The bride was dressed elegantly as she was on February 10, 1863, when she walked amid a similar throng in Grace Church to be married to General Tom Thumb.

60

Her robust little form was enveloped in a gown of lavender satin, brocaded in uncut velvet. It had a court train as long as the bride. The front was decked with lace, beaded with pearls. Cinderella slippers of lavender satin adorned her feet, which loosely fit a Number 6 infant shoe. A diamond necklace with a pendant glittered around her throat. Diamond bracelets sparkled at her wrists, and lavender kid gloves that reached nearly to her shoulders covered her shapely white hands and arms. The gloves were of a size known as 'four and a half infants' and they were made on a special block. In her left hand she carried a bouquet of pink La France roses that was much bigger than her head. Nobody who looked at her smiling face would have thought it possible she had passed her fortieth year. Silver-haired William Higby of Bridgeport, executor of General Tom Thumb's estate, took the bride's hand in his own big white-gloved palm and gave her away to the Count formally. The Count fitted the tiny wedding ring on the bride's finger with a daintiness that made the big throng of onlookers laugh audibly with pleasure. Then the Count imprinted a kiss on his bride's red lips, and tall Rector Watkins, stooping away over until it seemed to those in the back rows that he touched the floor, kissed the little woman, too. Then everybody beamed smiles upon the receding procession as they walked away."

A month later the Count and Countess went to the Count's home in Italy where they passed the summer. Upon their return to the United States they, with Baron Magri, made their headquarters at Lavinia's family home in Middleborough. The two little brothers were familiar figures on the streets of the town, strutting up and down the main street, dressed in black suits, tall silk hats, enormous cigars between their lips, slyly flirting with the girls. Countess Magri, who gained weight with the years and was, one could say, pleasingly plump, frequently made trips to the center of the town to shop or call on friends. Her conveyance was Billy Murphy's hack. Billy Murphy, a town character himself and beloved by all, owned and drove

Count Primo Magri, Countess Magri, Edward Newell (Minnie Warren's widower) the second Mrs. Newell, Baron Ernest Magri.

the town hack, meeting all trains and supplying the service of a modern day taxi. The hack was a closed vehicle with windows in the doors on either side of the cab. As Billy drove the Countess to town, she was much too short to be glimpsed through the windows, but she always wore a feather or egret in her bonnet. As the hack passed by and one saw a feathery ornament bobbing about inside, one knew the passenger was Countess Magri.

Lavinia maintained a close relationship with other members of the "small world" of which she and they were a part. Especially close were the two Adams sisters, Sarah and Lucy, both midgets who lived at Oak Bluffs on the island of Martha's Vineyard off Cape Cod. Sarah was Lavinia's bridesmaid when she married Count Magri. Sarah never grew to be taller than forty-six inches and Lucy never taller than forty-nine inches.

62

Mrs. Tom Thumb was responsible for the Adams sisters' theatrical career. When Lucy and her sister were in their teens they were in great demand as entertainers for church and other local affairs. The two girls were brought up to be strict Methodists and a stage career was farthest from their thoughts. One day the son of their church pastor, living in Plymouth, Massachusetts, sent a distress call to his father for some talent for a church social. The father immediately thought of his little parishioners who were so popular as entertainers in his own church.

The two sisters went to Plymouth and were enthusiastically received. Mrs. Tom Thumb, living only sixteen miles away, saw notices of the entertainment, and since she and the General were then managing their own company, wrote Mrs. Adams requesting that Sarah and Lucy come to Middleboro to discuss joining their company. The parents were not pleased at the prospect of a stage career for their daughters and it was not until a representative of the Tom Thumbs had made several trips to Oak Bluffs that a contract was signed. The only condition upon which the parents would allow their daughters to engage in theatrical appearances was that there be no Sunday bookings. The sisters adhered to this principal throughout their stage careers.

The sisters lived in what is known as "Cottage City," a community in Oak Bluffs of quaint gingerbread houses where the famous camp meetings were held each year and where each Fourth of July every house was ablaze with Japanese lanterns.

Sarah died in 1938, the result of an accident, but Lucy lived to be over ninety. In her ninetieth year she accepted an invitation to speak before the Middleborough Historical Association and in the cold and stormy month of November braved the ocean voyage on the crossing from Vineyard Haven to Woods Hole and arrived at the meeting vivacious and sparkling. She stood on the platform, scorning the use of a microphone and reminisced about her travels, her varied experiences, and her friendship with Mrs. Tom Thumb. At the close of the program in a firm, clear voice, she recited entirely from memory the complete poem, "Hiawatha's Wooing." Miss Adams died of pneumonia in December, 1954, in her ninety-third year.

Miss Lucy Adams, 90, chatting with Norman W. Lindsay, president of the Middleborough Historical Society, November 5, 1951.

SARAH AND LUCY ADAMS
When they were young women appearing on the stage

Another dear friend of Lavinia's was the tiny midget, Dolly Dutton. Dolly was born in Framingham, Massachusetts in 1852, into a normal sized family with the exception of one sister. The father, mother, two brothers and a sister were all of usual size, but one little sister never grew to be more than thirty inches in height, nor more than fifteen pounds in weight. The sister died at the age of eight years, but before her death the two little midgets made many public appearances together.

A relative of the family remembered seeing Mr. Dutton go down the aisle of a circus with arms outstretched, holding one in the palm of each hand, Dolly and her sister. A ring worn by Dolly fitted the finger of a year old infant and an oval bracelet that belonged to her scarcely encircled the finger of a normal sized person, looking more like a ring than a bracelet. A ticket to one of Dolly's exhibitions read, "Levee of the Little Fairy, Miss Dolly Dutton." A little sofa and side chair used by her could well serve as doll's furniture, measuring in height the length of a new lead pencil.

Dolly often traveled with the Tom Thumb troupe. At thirty years of age she was thirty-nine inches tall and weighed fifteen pounds. She married a normal sized man, Mr. B. Sarvin, and had a baby boy who weighed at birth one pound and two ounces, but who lived only a few hours. Dolly died in Natick, Massachusetts, on June 6, 1890, aged thirty-eight years.

Lavinia often expressed her intention to retire when she had completed fifty years before the public, but when that time arrived, she and the Count had just returned from two years of successful appearances in London and Paris. Then, too, their financial position made it advisable to continue public appearances as long as possible. Their earnings had been large. However they lived lavishly and spent freely, but not wisely. In their declining years they were forced to sell piece by piece the miniature furniture and most of the valuable gifts given them in such abundance in order to have money for everyday living expenses. Therefore, for several years the two brothers and the Countess continued to tour the vaudeville circuits. That they enjoyed little rest from stage work is indicated by items in the Middleboro Gazette as late as 1910, when the Countess was sixty-nine years of age:

"January 21, 1910. The Little Folk are now filling an engagement in a London theatre. It is expected that they will return about March 1st. Letters recently received indicate they are in excellent health.

"April 15, 1910. Count and Countess Magri assisted at an entertainment in Brockton Monday evening . . .

"December 2, 1910. The 'Little Folk' were at home for a few hours Sunday. They are making a tour of the New England states, beginning the week at Lowell, Massachusetts."

Their last public appearances were made at Coney Island, New York. The trio made a brief visit to Hollywood and appeared in a few moving pictures. At long last the discomforts of travel became too arduous for the three little troupers and they retired to Lavinia's family home in Middleborough.

A small roadside stand was constructed next to the home and named "Primo's Pastime." Here the three little people welcomed automobile tourists, selling them candy and soda pop, sharing their reminiscences with all who stopped. The opportunity to see and talk with the famous Mrs. Tom Thumb was much more of an inducement to stop than the desire for refreshments.

In their retirement, the little people were most generous in aiding worthy causes by presenting their entertainment of playlets and recitations, most of these performances taking place in the old Grand Army Hall on the second floor of historic Peirce Academy in Middleborough, a fond memory of those who can recall these presentations.

The Countess remained active to the end of her life. On her seventy-fourth birthday she dedicated a boulder to her ancestor, Richard Warren, of Revolutionary fame. The boulder was placed on the lawn of the family homestead, bearing the following inscription:

"In memory of Richard Warren and his descendants, In commemoration of my 74th birthday, October 31, 1915.

Countess Magri (Mrs. Tom Thumb)

COUNT AND COUNTESS MAGRI
Standing in front of Primo's Pasttime

The boulder remained on the lawn of the homestead until 1930 when the house was about to be sold. A close friend of the Countess, Mrs. Edith Finney, wished to have the boulder preserved. She obtained permission from the heirs to move it to a Memory Garden at Montgomery Home in Middleborough, of which Mrs. Finney was matron. In the early 1960's, the trustees of Montgomery Home planned to make changes in the landscaping of the grounds and the boulder was moved to the property of the Middleborough Historical Museum, where it now rests.

Although in her early years the Countess worshipped with her family at the First Congregational Church at the Green in Middleborough, she frequently attended the Christian Science Church in that town where a small chair was always kept in readiness for her in the front row of seats. She was a member of E. W. Post, G.A.R; Women's Relief Corps; Order of Eastern Star, the Golden Gate Chapter of San Francisco and an honorary member of thirteen other chapters including the Hannah Shaw Chapter of Middleborough; Nemasket Grange, P. of H.; a D.A.R. chapter of New York State and an honorary member of Deborah Sampson Chapter of Brockton, Massachusetts, and of Nemasket Chapter, Middleborough.

On October 31, 1919, the Countess felt sufficiently well to entertain over one hundred and fifty friends in celebration of her seventy-eighth birthday. In the following days her health deteriorated rapidly. She passed away at her home on November 25, 1919. Funeral services were held at the home conducted by the Reverend Arthur G. Cummings, pastor of the First Congregational Church and the Reverend Louis A. Walker, formerly minister of the Unitarian Church of Middleborough. The Countess was buried with her first husband, General Tom Thumb, in Mountain Grove Cemetery, Bridgeport, Connecticut.

The Countess' will requested that her collection of curios be held by a trustee to be appointed by the probate court for exhibition in a public or private museum. Legal technicalities made this impossible. At long last, the Middleborough Historical Museum is carrying out the last wishes of Countess Magri as expressed in her last will and testament and in her favorite poem, "Keep Me in Your Memory."

COUNT AND COUNTESS MAGRI
With bicycle on which the Count rode to town

69

COUNTESS MAGRI
In her later years

Chapter V
AMONG THEIR SOUVENIRS

Approximately a year after the Countess' death, on October 13th, 14th, and 15th, 1920, Count Magri held an auction at the family homestead on Plymouth Street, Middleborough, offering the pitifully few possessions left of all the costly presents lavished upon the four little people throughout their years of public life, hoping to realize enough money to enable him to return to his homeland. The Boston papers gave the auction considerable publicity and the sale was attended by antique and curio seekers from far and near. However, the articles did not bring the high prices expected and in the Boston Globe of October 15, 1920 appeared the following account of the auction:

"TOM THUMB EFFECTS BROUGHT ABOUT $1000
OIL PAINTINGS WERE NOT SOLD, SO AS TO GIVE
MIDDLEBORO A CHANCE TO PRESERVE THEM

The last of the furniture and curios of the late General Tom Thumb were sold at auction yesterday, and when late in the afternoon, auctioneer William Egger, closed the sale there had been less than $1000 received for the goods that in their days were considered almost priceless.

Most of the articles were sold except four large paintings of Tom Thumb and his wife, who was afterwards known as Countess Magri, her midget sister Minnie Warren, and another midget Commodore Nutt.

71

These were about to be sold at auction and several dealers on hand were ready to give them a good start, but Mr. William Egger, the auctioneer of Middleboro, made a proposition that he would hold them and take a chance that the town would buy them . . .

The bidding yesterday was not so spirited as on Wednesday and most of the articles sold were of value simply as curios and keepsakes from the Tom Thumb collection.

THE TOM THUMB AUCTION
October, 1920

MINIATURE PIANO AT SMITHSONIAN INSTITUTION
Never owned by Tom Thumb but said to have been used by him
in his presentations.

The little sewing machine and cabinet went for $27.50; the little parlor sofa for $15.00; a tiny easy chair for $6.00; a parlor table for $15.00; while the pool table with cues, billiard balls and all the fittings went for $31.00.

Several pictures were sold as low as $1.00, while medals specially struck off for Tom Thumb in some European countries sold as low as 50 cents.

Count Magri, in whose interest the auction was held, will remain until spring, when he will sail for Bologna, Italy. He has no definite plans for the future and says he may come back to this country if his health improves."

Mr. Elmer Drew, an antique dealer of Middleborough, was one of the heaviest bidders. Among his purchases was the little grand piano given the Tom Thumbs by Queen Victoria. Mr. Drew's bid of $11.00 bought it. He placed the instrument in his antique shop. Not long afterward a gentleman came in to browse about. He purchased items amounting to about eighteen dollars and then casually inquired, "How much for the toy piano?" Then Mr. Drew knew the prime purpose of the visit was to purchase the Tom Thumb piano. "Two hundred dollars," said Mr. Drew. At first feigning surprise that a toy piano should command such a high price, the customer paid it, obviously delighted with his purchase. The buyer proved to be the owner of large New England woolen mills.

Having heard that the Smithsonian Institution in Washington, D.C. included among its exhibits a small grand piano that very well might be the Tom Thumb piano, the author journeyed to Washington to investigate. Located in the section of Musical Instruments and Division of Cultural History, the little piano was beautifully displayed on a raised platform. Made of glistening black wood, it was decorated with an ornamental gilt molding. In answer to her queries, the author received the following information in writing:

"According to our records, this piano was built by Kirkman & Son of London, especially for the Crystal Palace Exhibition in 1851. Built so that every detail of a large grand was reproduced in miniature, it is said to have been used by Tom Thumb on his exhibition tours. The piano was given the Smithsonian in 1920 by Hugo Worck, a Washington piano dealer who presented a large keyboard collection to the Smithsonian. We have no record of where Mr. Worck purchased this piano nor any formal documents that verify the Tom Thumb collection.

Signed,
Richard M. Howland, Chairman,
Dept. of Civil History,
Smithsonian Institution.

It is extremely regrettable and an everlasting indictment of the indifference and apathy of the citizens of Mrs. Tom Thumb's home town that no effort was made to retain these priceless possessions. The one public effort to keep any of the possessions in Middleborough was that put forth by Mr. Egger, the auctioneer, when he bid in the four life-sized portraits of General and Mrs. Tom Thumb, Minnie Warren, and Commodore Nutt. These likenesses are said to have been photographs taken in London, blown up to life size and painted in oils so that they have every appearance of being oil portraits. The canvas was cracked and the frames in very poor condition. Mr. Egger placed a notice in the Middleboro Gazette asking for contributions toward having the paintings and frames restored. It was thought fifty dollars would be sufficient to pay for the work. Contributions of $34.00 were received and Mr. Egger made up the balance. Mrs. J. Herbert Cushing, a local artist, restored the paintings and their handsome gilt frames. On October 3, 1921, there was a ceremony of considerable pomp and circumstance in the Middleborough Town Hall at which time the paintings were formally presented to the Town of Middleborough, after which they were hung in the Middleboro Public Library, where they may be seen today.

In 1927, when the Bump homestead, the last home of the little folk, was on the market to be sold, a second auction was held of the few remaining articles that had belonged to the Tom Thumbs. The bids were surprisingly low and only a small group of bidders attended. A little musket and bayonet used

GENERAL TOM THUMB
"American Man in Miniature"

76

MRS. TOM THUMB
A favorite picture

by Tom Thumb in some of his stage characterizations was sold for $23.50; a pair of the Countess' gloves, $3.00; a little chair, $5.25; a collection of buttons gathered by the Countess and Minnie Warren in their world travels, $6.00; a picture of the Countess when twenty years old, $17.50; a tea set of willow ware, $30.00; an ivory elephant, "Baby Jumbo," presented by P. T. Barnum, $12.50; a little brass bed with four curved rods forming a canopy topped by a crown, brought no bids at all. The entire proceeds of the auction netted only $300.00.

The author attended both auctions and as the present curator of the Middleborough Historical Museum, recognizes several gifts to the Museum's Tom Thumb Collection as items purchased at one of the auctions.

Only two weeks after the first auction in 1920, Count Magri was stricken fatally ill. In failing health and with almost no money, his last days were sad and lonely. His brother, the Baron, had died in Boston a short time before the Count's death. The Count died at St. Luke's Hospital in Middleborough on October 31, 1920, in his seventy-second year, and on the seventy-ninth birthday anniversary of the Countess.

Funeral services for the last of the little folk were held at the home of one who had been a loyal friend, Mr. William Egger. Bearers represented the Middleboro Lodge of the Benevolent Order of Elks. Interment was in St. Mary's Cemetery, Middleborough.

The family homestead in Warrentown where Lavinia and Minnie and the other little folk spent so much of their time has been sold and remodeled, bearing no resemblance to the comfortable white farmhouse with its wide porches and broad shady lawns, the home from which Lavinia and Minnie so gaily set forth on careers that took them around the world and brought them fame and fortune.

Possessions of the Tom Thumbs are to be found in museums throught the country:

SUTRO'S MUSEUM, SEAL ROCKS,
SAN FRANCISCO, CALIFORNIA

A large collection including some of the Tom Thumb furniture, glass cases filled with clothing worn by the four little people, a diminutive kitchen stove from their home in Middleborough, a fishing creel with a label reading, "Used by Tom Thumb when fishing in the Nemasket River at Middleborough," and the prize possessions, one of the black coaches in which General and Mrs. Tom Thumb rode, and the gilded walnut-shell coach built especially for Commodore Nutt.

RINGLING CIRCUS MUSEUM, SARASOTA, FLORIDA

Several small articles including one of the wedding pictures, a leather vest worn by Tom Thumb, one of his small canes, Lavinia's wedding handkerchief, a metal belt. In a sep arate exhibition is one of the Tom Thumb coaches.

HENRY FORD MUSEUM, DEARBORN, MICHIGAN

Pool table, a wedding gift, beautifully carved, 18 inches high, bearing a silver plate stating the table was made by Phelan & Collander & Company, of New York and San Francisco. Purchased by the Museum from Carroll & Co., Hyannis, Massachusetts, Feb. 6, 1941. A miniature velocipede, 18 inches high with wooden wheels having metal rims, presented to Tom Thumb by the makers, Topliff & Ely, Elyria, Ohio. One of the black coaches in which General and Mrs. Tom Thumb rode, and like so many of the other coaches, claiming to be the one presented by Queen Victoria. There were several of the little black coaches stationed at various strategic points about the United States to be available when the Tom Thumb troupe was putting on their entertainment in that part of the country.

It is very likely that the coach presented by Queen Victoria is no longer in existence. At least none of those extant coincide with the description published at the time of the presentation to Tom Thumb. Newspaper accounts stated the coach was manufactured by S. Beaton of No. 16 Denmark Street, Soho, London (Carriage manufacturer to the Queen). A description as printed at that time states:

"It is an elegant Dress Chariot, 20 inches high and 12 inches wide, completely furnished in the richest style with every requisite, lined with a rich figured yellow silk lace to match; Venetian shutters, plate glass and spring roller blinds. The colour is an ultra marine blue, elegantly picked out with crimson and

79

white; the body hangs upon black patent leather braces, beautifully worked in white silk . . . Upon the door panels, and also on the back and front panels, are emblazoned the arms, the Goddess of Liberty and Britannia, in a double shield, supported by the American Eagle and Rampant Lion, crest, the rising sun, with the American and British flags crossed, the motto, 'Go-a-head.' "

The coach at Dearborn is of gleaming black wood, standing approximately 36 inches high and 6 feet in length, with an elevated seat high in front for the little coachman. The entire front of the carriage is a curved glass window, curtained in crimson draperies. The doors have windows that may be lowered. The interior is upholstered in a rich red plush.

Regarding this coach, the "History of New Hampshire" states:

> "This coach was made in England and was presented to Mr. and Mrs. Tom Thumb by Queen Victoria. It had been presented to the university of New Hampshire in 1922 by William G. Smalley of Walpole, New Hampshire, in honor of his son, Maxwell W. Smalley of the class of 1917. The coach has been placed by action of the trustees of the college in Henry Ford's Museum in Dearborn, Michigan."

THE P. T. BARNUM MUSEUM,
BRIDGEPORT, CONNECTICUT
Clothing and accessories used by Tom Thumb.

BRIDGEPORT PUBLIC LIBRARY,
BRIDGEPORT, CONNECTICUT
HENRY A. BISHOP MEMORIAL ROOM

A visiting card of Tom Thumb's, measuring one by two inches; a plaster cast of his tiny foot and a pair of his boots; one of his tall silk hats, six inches tall; the court dress worn by his generalship when first presented to Queen Victoria at Buckingham Palace in 1844; an embroidered shirt; a luxurious housecoat of red velvet.

80

THE MIDDLEBOROUGH HISTORICAL MUSEUM, MIDDLEBOROUGH, MASSACHUSETTS

It would be impossible to enumerate the large number of articles that belonged to the small quartet on display in the Middleborough Historical Museum. There are four rooms filled to capacity, comprising what is probably the largest collection of Tom Thumb memorabilia. Of especial interest are: the black jet dress with long train worn by Lavinia when presented to Queen Victoria; several other dresses, including dainty party dresses worn when she was a young woman; an intricately carved set of small table and chairs made of teakwood, presented to Tom Thumb by the Emperor of Japan; a very small chariot and horse wrought of filigree silver, embellished with colored stones, a wedding gift from the jewelers, Tiffany of New York. Originally the stones were real gems — garnets and rubies — but when in their later years the couple found themselves in straightened circumstances, they removed the genuine stones, sold them, and replaced them with paste jewels. A piece of the wedding cake distributed to guests at the wedding reception of Tom Thumb and Lavinia; a silver tea set made by a local jeweler, Charles Carpenter, and presented to Lavinia who refused to accept it because the set was decorated with horses and goats, considered unlucky in the circus. Several small canes carried by General Tom Thumb and one of his tiny silk hats; several pairs of tiny gloves and slippers worn by Lavinia and Minnie; a copy of the Tom Thumb Wedding March, composed by E. Mack; a copy of the "Tom Thumb Polka," lyrics by Edna Bump, music by Henry B. Burkland.

With the exception of a small collection purchased from Benjamin Bump, a nephew of Mrs. Tom Thumb, every article in the Tom Thumb Collection has been a gift to the Museum. Many people are glad to have a safe haven for a Tom Thumb possession that has been in the family for years and might not be preserved by a younger generation.

The Executive Board of the Middleborough Historical Museum welcomes all such gifts, appreciative of the fact that these souvenirs are poignant reminders of four little people who may not have been the smallest midgets ever known, but were seen by more people, appeared before more members of royalty, and will remain longer in the memory of the world than any other individuals of comparable size.

Standing: Benjamin Warren Bump, (Mrs. Tom Thumb's brother), Sylvester Bleeker (manager of Tom Thumb Company), Mrs. Bleeker, George Willis Bump (another brother). Front row: Mrs. Tom Thumb, General Tom Thumb, Minnie Warren.

CHAPTER VI
Concerning General and Mrs. Tom Thumb
and some other midgets

The middle 1800's was a time for small paper covered books on a variety of subjects. Religious tracts were especially popular, and several publishers took advantage of the trend to publish small booklets about the "life, personal appearance, character, and manners" of General Tom Thumb and his wife Lavinia. These also included information about "remarkable dwarfs, giants, and other human phenomena," both ancient and modern.

The first few pages of the booklets were usually devoted to dwarfs who had lived in early days as well as those of more modern times. Members of royalty were especially interested in these small bits of humanity and had one or two in their entourage. It is said Julia, favorite wife of Emporer Augustus, had a devoted dwarf named Sonapas who was two feet seven inches in height.

Quoting from one of the booklets published by Van Norden & Amerman of New York in 1867:

"Geoffrey Hudson, the most celebrated dwarf in English history and the only one comparable with the subject of this memoir, lived in the reign of Charles the Second and was attached to the court of that monarch. At full maturity his height was three feet nine inches, but when seven or eight years old, such was his diminutive proportion that he was set upon the king's table in a large dish of pastry from which he emerged

SKETCH

OF THE

LIFE, PERSONAL APPEARANCE, CHARACTER AND MANNERS

OF

CHARLES S. STRATTON,

THE MAN IN MINIATURE, KNOWN AS

GENERAL TOM THUMB,

AND HIS WIFE,

LAVINIA WARREN STRATTON,

INCLUDING THE HISTORY OF THEIR

COURTSHIP AND MARRIAGE,

WITH SOME ACCOUNT OF

Remarkable Dwarfs, Giants, & other Human Phenomena,

OF ANCIENT AND MODERN TIMES.

ALSO,

SONGS GIVEN AT THEIR PUBLIC LEVEES

NEW YORK:

PRESS OF WYNKOOP & HALLENBECK,

No. 113 FULTON STREET.

1867.

One of the several booklets about the Tom Thumbs, their court-
ship, marriage, and stage appearances.

84

to the amusement of the company as soon as the crust was broken. He was taken into the service of the Queen during which period he challenged and shot a young nobleman in a duel, and finally died in prison where he had been confined for a political offense.

In our own day, Count Borwalaski was the greatest little man. He was very little, very amiable and very accomplished, but he was head and shoulders higher than General Tom Thumb. Count Borwalaski, like the General, was a special favorite of royalty, for he frequently visited George the Fourth . . ."

Teresa, called the Corsican Fairy because of her place of birth, and born in 1743, was noted for her physical beauty and her intellectual talents. Only thirty-eight inches in height, she was said to be charming in conversation and spoke several languages. When exhibited in London she created a great furore of excitement.

General Tom Thumb's Family Party.

GENERAL TOM THUMB'S FAMILY PARTY
As it appeared in the booklet published by Wynkoop & Hallenbeck, N. Y., 1867.

SENORITA LUCIA ZARATE
The Mexican Lilliputian

The Mexican Lilliputian, Senorita Lucia Zarate, was called the "Greatest Wonder of the Age." On the back of her picture is written: This young lady is thirteen years of age and twenty inches high. Is perfect in form and features. Tom Thumb is a giant beside this wonderful Mexican pigmy. It would be difficult to exaggerate the wonders of this human curiosity. The plain truth makes it strange enough." Lucia died in 1899 of pneumonia as a result of exposure while on a train stalled by a blizzard in the Sierra Nevada mountains.

86

ADMIRAL DOT
Smaller (and handsomer) than Tom Thumb

Admiral Dot was the son of Gabriel Kahn, a San Franciscan German. The Admiral could speak both German and English and was even smaller (and handsomer) than Tom Thumb. Barnum discovered him in San Francisco and was clever enough to make him appear even smaller by exhibiting him with Colonel Goshen, an Arabian giant. Like Tom Thumb, Admiral Dot traveled many seasons under Barnum's auspices. He finally settled down in 1897 as the owner of a pub in White Plains, New York.

GENERAL MITE
The Greatest Wonder of the Nineteenth century

On the back of General Mite's photograph is printed:
A HUMAN MIRACLE
GENERAL MITE
assuredly the
SMALLEST MAN IN THE WORLD
He is
12 years of age
22 inches high
and weighs
ONLY 9 POUNDS
This little gentleman weighed only two and
one-half pounds at birth, and grew to his
present size the first year of his life. He is
remarkably handsome and perfect in form
and feature, is bright, active, and intelligent,
and is, no doubt
THE GREATEST WONDER OF THE
NINETEENTH CENTURY

Major Stevens, the first midget to be exhibited in America,
was about forty inches in height and an accomplished gentleman. He was exhibited in almost every state in the Union and,
until Tom Thumb appeared on the scene, was considered a most
remarkable midget, but when Tom Thumb first joined the exhibits at the American Museum, beside him Major Stevens
looked a giant, being nearly twice the height and four times
the weight of the General.

Again quoting from the previously mentioned booklet as
it refers to General Tom Thumb: "Other dwarfs, of about the
same dimensions, male and female, have been exhibited within
a few years and regarded with no little wonder and curiosity.
Many of these tiny people have been much or partially de-
formed, and so pain has been felt whilst looking at them. But
in the case of the hero of our narrative, no such drawbacks
exist, even to the appearance of a defect. All former dwarfs
were, in shape as in size, inferior."

There is a difference between a dwarf and a midget. A
dwarf is of small stature and his head and torso may be of
normal proportions but his arms and legs are much too small,
whereas a midget ceases growing in early childhood but is
perfectly proportioned — truly men and women in miniature.

All are brought together in an organization known as "The Little People of America," headquartered in Owatonna, Minnesota. A dwarf named Billy Barty, familiar to many because of his appearance in motion pictures, started the organization in 1957, and it now has nearly 2,500 members. Anyone under four feet ten inches may join. Their motto is, "Think Big." There are regional conferences where the little people may meet others of like size and discuss mutual problems. Sometimes romance blossoms resulting in the ringing of wedding bells. The L.P.A. advises its members: A small person can live in two worlds — a small world and a normal world. A person who finds happiness in both worlds has nothing to lose to society or himself . . .

General and Mrs. Tom Thumb enjoyed the privilege of living in both worlds. They loved the companionship of people their own size and basked in the admiration and affection of their public.

COMMODORE NUTT
From the booklet published by Wynkoop & Hallenbeck, N.Y., 1867.

From the booklet published by Wynkoop & Hallenbeck, N.Y., 1867.

Besides giving information about other dwarfs, midgets, the life and character of the Tom Thumbs, and excerpts from newspapers extolling the charm and accomplishments of this pint size couple, these booklets also contain songs and recitations used by the small quartet in their entertainments. One pamphlet gives in entirety the play "Hop-O-My-Thumb, or Seven League Boots," a two act play written by Albert Smith expressly for Tom Thumb and presented by him in his stage appearances. Among the poems is Mrs. Tom Thumb's favorite and the one she most often recited in public and at private parties:

THEN YOU'LL REMEMBER ME

When other lips and other hearts
 Their tales of love shall tell,
In language where excess imparts
 The powers they feel so well;
There may, perhaps, in such a scene,
 Some recollection be,
Of days that have as happy been —
 Then you'll remember me.

When coldness or deceit shall fly,
 The beauties now I prize,
Or deem it but a faded light,
 That beams within your eyes;
When hollow hearts shall wear a mask,
 'Twill break your heart to see;
In such a moment I but ask
 That you'll remember me.

GENERAL AND MRS TOM THUMB AT THEIR
WEDDING RECEPTION
As pictured in the booklet published by Wynkoop & Hallenbeck,
N.Y., 1867.

CHRONOLOGY

GENERAL TOM THUMB   (Charles Sherwood Stratton)
Born: Bridgeport, Connecticut, January 4, 1838
Married: Mercy Lavinia Bump, February 10, 1863
Died: Middleborough, Massachusetts, July 15, 1883
Burial: Mountain Grove Cemetery, Bridgeport, Connecticut

MRS. TOM THUMB   (Mercy Lavinia Warren Bump)
Born: Middleborough, Massachusetts, October 31, 1841
Married: Charles S. Stratton, February 10, 1863
         Count Primo Magri, April 6, 1885
Died: Middleborough, Massachusetts, November 25, 1919
Burial: Mountain Grove Cemetery, Bridgeport, Connecticut

Minnie Warren   (Huldah Pierce Bump)
Born: Middleborough, Massachusetts, June 2, 1842
Married: Edward Newell, July, 1877
Died: Middleborough, Massachusetts, July 23, 1878
Burial: Nemasket Hill Cemetery, Middleborough, Mass.

Count Primo Magri
Born: Bologna, Italy, December 31, 1849
Married: Mercy Lavinia (Bump) Stratton, April 6, 1885
Died: Middleborough, Massachusetts, October 31, 1920
Burial: St. Mary's Cemetery, Middleborough, Mass.

SOURCE MATERIAL

P. T. Barnum — **Life of P. T. Barnum, 1854**

P. T. Barnum — **Struggles & Triumphs, 1871**

Sylvester Bleeker — **General Tom Thumb's Three Years Tour Around The World, 1872**

Elsie N. Danenberg — **Story of Bridgeport, 1936**

Mrs. Charles S. Stratton — **Diary** (Incomplete)

L. Sashton Thorp — **Manchester of Yesterday, 1939**

M. R. Werner — **Barnum, 1923**

J. H. Beers & Co., Chicago, Publishers — **Representative Men and Old Families of Southeastern Massachusetts, v. 3, 1912**

Pioneer Show Printing Co., Seattle, Washington, Publisher — **Mrs. General Tom Thumb, n.d.**

Van Norden & Amerman, New York, N. Y., Publisher — **Sketch of the Life, Personal Appearance, Character and Manners of Charles S. Stratton, the Man in Miniature, known as General Tom Thumb, 1847**

Wynkoop, Hallenbeck & Thomas, New York, N. Y., Publisher — **Same as above, 1860**

Wynkoop & Hallenbeck, New York, N. Y., Publisher — **Sketch of the Life, Personal Appearance, Character and Manners of Charles S. Stratton or General Tom Thumb and his wife, Lavinia Warren, 1867**

Newspapers consulted:
Boston Sunday Globe, July 20, 1975
Cosmopolitan Magazine, January 27, 1947
Middleborough Gazette and Old Colony Advertiser
Middleboro Gazette
Standard Times, New Bedford, Massachusetts
Providence, R. I., Journal